Pebble™

Dogs

Pugs

by Jody Sullivan Rake

Consulting Editor: Gail Saunders-Smith, PhD

Consultant: Jennifer Zablotny, DVM
Member, American Veterinary Medical Association

Capstone
press
Mankato, Minnesota

Pebble Books are published by Capstone Press,
151 Good Counsel Drive, P.O. Box 669, Mankato, Minnesota 56002.
www.capstonepress.com

1 2 3 4 5 6 11 10 09 08 07 06

Library of Congress Cataloging-in-Publication Data
Rake, Jody Sullivan.
    Pugs / by Jody Sullivan Rake.
    p. cm.—(Pebble Books. Dogs)
    Summary: "Simple text and photographs present an introduction to the pug
breed, its growth from puppy to adult, and pet care information"—Provided by
publisher.
    Includes bibliographical references and index.
    ISBN-13: 978-0-7368-5336-1 (hardcover)
    ISBN-10: 0-7368-5336-7 (hardcover)
    1. Pug. I. Title. II. Series.
SF429.P9R35 2006
636.76—dc22   2005023800

Note to Parents and Teachers

The Dogs set supports national science standards related to life
science. This book describes and illustrates pugs. The images
support early readers in understanding the text. The repetition of
words and phrases helps early readers learn new words. This book
also introduces early readers to subject-specific vocabulary words,
which are defined in the Glossary section. Early readers may need
assistance to read some words and to use the Table of Contents,
Glossary, Read More, Internet Sites, and Index sections of the book.

Table of Contents

Brave Dogs

Pugs are brave dogs.
They are not afraid
of much, even though
they are small.

Some pugs have jobs.
They go to hospitals
and nursing homes
to cheer people up.

From Puppy to Adult

Two to five pug puppies are born in each litter.

Pug puppies like
to play and chew.
Chew toys help make
their teeth strong.

Adult pugs are small, strong dogs.
They are as big as a large cat.

Pugs have short fur and a curly tail. Their faces are flat and wrinkled.

Taking Care of Pugs

Owners need to keep their pugs' faces clean. Dirt can get into the wrinkles.

Pugs are house dogs.
They need to live indoors
and be warm and dry.

Pugs need food, water, and exercise every day to stay healthy.
Love from their owners keeps them happy.

Glossary

cheer—to make someone glad or happy

curly—curved into a circle

exercise—physical activity and movement done to stay healthy

hospital—a place where doctors and nurses help sick and hurt people

nursing home—a place where people live so that nurses and caregivers can take care of them

wrinkle—a line or crease; pugs have lots of wrinkles on their faces.

Read More

Clutton-Brock, Juliet. *Dog.* DK Eyewitness Books. New York: Dorling Kindersley, 2004.

Hubbard, Woodleigh Marx. *For the Love of a Pug.* New York: G.P. Putnam's Sons, 2003.

Internet Sites

FactHound offers a safe, fun way to find Internet sites related to this book. All of the sites on FactHound have been researched by our staff.

Here's how:

1. Visit *www.facthound.com*
2. Type in this special code **0736853367** for age-appropriate sites. Or enter a search word related to this book for a more general search.
3. Click on the **Fetch It** button.

FactHound will fetch the best sites for you!

Index

Word Count: 128
Grade: 1
Early-Intervention Level: 14

Editorial Credits
Martha E. H. Rustad, editor; Juliette Peters, designer; Wanda Winch, photo researcher; Scott Thoms, photo editor

Photo Credits
Corbis/Tim Davis, cover; Elite Portrait Design/Lisa Fallenstein-Holthaus, 6, 16, 18; Kent Dannen, 14; Mark Raycroft, 1, 4, 8, 20; Norvia Behling, 10; Ron Kimball Stock/Ron Kimball, 12